Twilight

Javier RJ

lunar eclipses can mean transformation
a clearing of services no longer in use to you
in turn, to shine a light from within
we all stem from zodiacs, which signify purpose
to create something in goodness for ourselves
let this be a foundation to build empires upon
as you trust whatever unfolds in life as natural
and accept changes in knowing
this is all for a higher purpose

also by Javier Rhoden

Luminescence
Lamentations
Altschmerz

synopsis

love isn't a rabbit hole to get lost in
it's rather mountainous with various peaks and dead ends
patience alongside endurance is what's needed to climb it
in observance to surroundings, so some things
you don't have to live through, the more insight you have
the less someone can persuade how you don't
why experience a world without studying details
seen from the vessel you see it through?

this is when perception fornicated with reality
after realizing, people in proximity won't be close to you
those thought of to be different had ill desires
with alternate approaches
it's easy to feel odd in a world convinced it's even
still, it gets nowhere recycling similar encounters
with different demons

relationships may grieve like broken hearts upon sleeves
but rifts are creations to openings, opportunities
won't squeeze through locked shackles, this is why
having no company is better
than engaging the wrong company
there's no community without unity
there's no association without unification of self, neglect this
existence will remain disfigured with viewpoints in a shelter

unchain from lifelines to outside sources
nothing has a hold on you because life
isn't dependent on who the heart clings to
it's dependent on levels in awareness of self
given your circumstances
regardless of how others have treated you

everything internal projects outward
let everything to break out in freeness be of positivity

following fame.

they know more about the lives of people
unaware of theirs
while those within the environment
walk beside each other in portals of loneliness

listen.

how could you love me
if those ears pick up
every sound around us, except this one
in a scream for you to help keep me
grounded

demons.

only a demon desires to confine you
to the lack of possibilities
in saying you can never amount to anything

your success and self preservation
will be more effective than holy water

boxed up.

love is a gift with double standards
pain is the bowtie
it's presented like happiness
but to create your own will leave you in aloneness
because hate was tucked into creased edges
of boxes their version of love
was only to keep you encased in

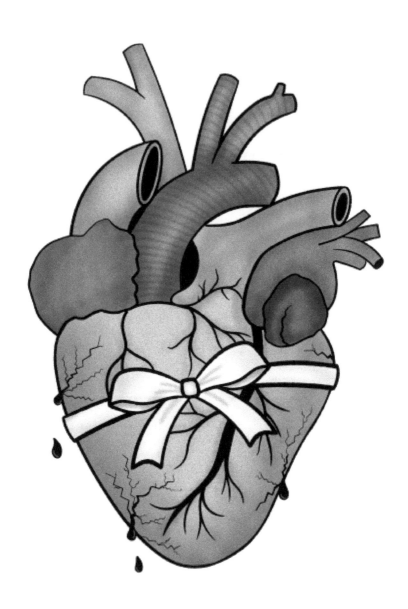

grit.

feel pain long enough
you begin to wake into death
you can see on my face i'm a walking mess
but my eyes
these eyes shine secrets of the grit it takes
to keep moving

imagine how powerful you become
upon acknowledging how far you've come
when someone else
would have succumbed to nothingness
on roads to paradise

a new day.

some days, to rise
it feels like suppression
upon what moves me
other days, to fall
it feels like rest embraces me
because nothing moves me

companionship.

it isn't until pain becomes a daily companion
that you decide to emotionally
check out of the relationship, funny though
how we carry on those lessons
as if decades were scaled back to seconds

abyss.

to live is to wade through
an abyss of what has ended
how else do you enjoy a life
without fear?

feeding the soul comes with a price
in this world asleep
to the fact that happiness comes free

you piece of shit.

the average person doesn't look back
at feces to call it a "piece of shit"
before every flush

so why won't you believe me
when i say they only degrade
what's already valuable?

there's no shine without a little grind
so survive the process
and thrive

respect.

no matter amounts of pressure, physical pain
has never crippled your mind frame
what makes you believe
a switch in method can bring different results?

wrath is the fire to burn through limitations without hesitation
pain has shaken apologies
from every bone used to pulverize senseless judgment
honor was impressed in demeanor that demands attention
even in silence

respect has always traveled through two way tunnels
but there are those who will make it their one way highway
their need for validation is the lowest valley to leave their corpses
the only esteem you ever need is remembrance
from what you've overcome

greatness.

when it feels crippling
envision your situation to be the best case scenario
and remain grateful

it could be worse
it could be a different realm of hell kind of worse

courage is in few
not everyone exercises consistency
but you do

only the strong survive

choices.

some people second guess decisions
only to wonder why they feel forsaken
doubt is the robber of blessings refused to be taken in
this feels suffocating and they look to a hero for saving
the one with self application for motivation
only to sink a ship not meant to uphold people and their burdens

their only elevation is to recognize
they're a fire blazing
but to become extinguished to light another flame
is a realm of self sacrifice
if you couldn't save yourself
then why does self come with a lifetime
of choices?

martyr.

to feel in need is to realize
you've been taking from yourself with no replenishment
upon sinking further into the depths of death
are you truly a victim?

how does your belief system not cause
this kind of self destruct?

remember everything constructed outside
busted from life within

energy.

this life feels injected with illusions, the more
my focus stays shifted on me
are when people and things
no longer fit into perfect lines of what they seem

i've seen them hunt down counterparts
or possessions as energy sources like vampires
yet desire never speaks quieter
a little too much of anything takes them out of themselves
but won't ever question what they're feeding

set boundaries towards what's ingested
and watch the frauds stifle
before dying off

word is bond.

words transitioned depthless
like a plagiarist without identity
an entity of all powerful creation
but in limitation from introspection

discussed arrangements without mindful engagement
were like business deals when they fell through
you were left in view as one with loose screws
when it took asking for assistance to understand
closest people will watch you
bleed through pavements walked on to find the greater you
there couldn't be togetherness if mindfulness
wasn't their business
desertion of emotions to leave consciousness
at the forefront, was result

survivability was uncovered
in lost and founds of cold shoulders
hurt was the only way to apply self love
although hate infiltrated, it never penetrated
don't be a breeding ground for replication
expectation was set up for disappointment
love knows no coldness like touch upon steel
it's why word is bond

sacrifices.

circumstances tend to snowball, as if it's
a natural course to go downward after moves upward
walks towards independence
may bring you to a crossroad, do you
place food to grace on a table
or fund visions to your version of a bigger picture?

bills accumulate on a life on street corners of sacrifices
street lights blow out like light bulbs to your future
time neglects no minute when living
has you on simmer like a slow cooker

this becomes lifestyle that's strenuous to uphold
survival becomes your biggest motivation
upon realizing accountability
won't come from a separate mentality
i see why dreams stay dormant the older we age
taking beneficial risk has everything to do with inner love
learn to manage stress in maintenance of composure
dispersed energy loops to find you right back
so get your thought process acclimated
for when it's next up, you can step up
efforts aren't in vain if you remain in the game
in no rush, as you focus on what's in your control
through these shifts, watch everything fall into place

power of responsibility.

in voice of a gps
life presented a left turn off main street
roads of opportunity lead to dead ends
how could one know where to go
without ears in pickup of static from holy whispers?
every u-turn was a mistuned plea of disbelief
to be helped in unbelief
despite staying in motion
improvement didn't budge, as you questioned
if you were being taught perseverance
or perhaps mistakes were being revealed?
these times felt farthest from an omniscient god
who often kept directions mysterious

certainty was the vehicle in slippage
of rear wheels in rainfall
impact of collision spiked decibels of chaos
loud, like chants from lies in your head
in protest of game over

yet faith were taken in as breaths of life
the blind led unconsciousness to artificial light
mass followers weren't prosperous in dynamic lifestyles
daily was the battle of deception
mentally, spiritually, physically
through a better mindset, do you remain in control
to what's in your grasp and explore new routes?
or do you believe god turns the key
with a foot on the pedal and a passenger seat
tailored for you? it can't be both
placement of responsibility is your choice though

power of now.

from outlooks of compassion, it was a challenge
to see human beings, instead stars were seen
so heavy, they suspended from homes in skies
explicit lullabies dispersed when darkness invaded light
this kind of impact created breaches in time, a crime
for laziness wasn't fashioned into souls by design

each day was spent avoiding explosions
from irreconcilable placements of landmines
it was easy to lose track of transitions to daytime
when demeanors lacked expression from a love within
it was harder to create space for more additions
upon feeling helpless, neglected breathless in states of stress
but rising to step up through lowest benchmarks
raised a level in how deep you fell the next time

remember, when acting in the power of now
you're charged in resilience

undervalued.

"how did you learn to let things go?" she asked

"i was casted to a wilderness but observed strength
in how leaves rained from forgiving trees
this was captivation in newness
like birth from bare branches to fullness
i saw how humans too
could shed through seasons in life
yet remain in glory of oneness

we were created to thrive, sometimes it was seen later
callous in development from hanging on for too long
was formed while assembling futile egos
one day while being lost in thought
realization spoke and revealed
we sometimes drank and partook in drugs
to soothe underlying pain of self-infliction
with desires in roam to get hired"
he whispered

temperamental.

what flowed from mouths were contradictions
hardness of stone settled in tones of voices
the very grounds of their pebbled surface
were stiff like jabs, hence why smiles of promises
often resembled broken gutters of abandoned houses

reminder to self:
thickened skin was byproduct
of no longer making assumptions
or taking things personal
all dependability enforced on another
was invested within
it's impossible to be ready for every problem faced
yet engage with an open mind
in due time, movements become different
if you want better, then be better
to be better is to know better
don't wait for situations to leave you clueless
to teach how implementation of knowledge is powerful
fertilize the mind with information while the soul is in liberation
without instances of confidence in depreciation
is what to tell yourself without giving in to persuasions

from a fallout with someone
it's best to part ways to learn how to crawl again
out of others, to walk deeper into yourself
this is spiritual vibration

reminders.

i.
when nightfall elongates
thoughts flood in nanoseconds, observe these waves
change is manifestation from action
movements reveal intention at forefront
so find strength to come around like sunrise
when progression has slowed
remember, staying in motion will reveal a destination

ii.
in vulnerability of your birthday suit
skin will soften in purpose
when putting on compositions of woven fabric
remember to minimize amounts of time
spent on rationalizing situations
there's always healthier perspectives to pick up on
you have no life without breath
if we are words we speak, everything out spoken
has identity to drive force behinds beats
so rhythms reflect california fires within, in its entirety
for this kind of love should never be mistreated

remain unmoved ii.

you have chandeliers in shine
like clusters in south side of your eyes
we all have afternoons of downpours, it'll slow
light travels through rays to find pockets of cheeks
despite washed out trails on your beautiful face

it's in upward stretches of lip muscles
you're reminded it gets better
speak positivity in face of negativity
and smile
you're persevering

discernment.

it's no secret people will desert you
this is why you can't quit on yourself
use darkened days as advantage
like a thief in nighttime
break in to reclaim consolation of reality
just as we entered this world alone
that's how we'll leave it, like looseness in happiness
in escape with pixie dust
relationships may be walks of companionship
but it's important to tie your own laces before hikes
she may just watch you trip before denying ill motives

uncontrolled actions resonated lower in frequency
as a man, self-control should be priority
letters from durability advised
how to bounce back with potential
to give one hundred percent with more discernment
in avoidance of another loss they called breakup

no more suffocating yourself
trying to be someone else's oxygen
wasted love notes transitioned to maps
for experiences wanted next time

compromise.

i.
vitality surged more freely than blood flow
it was in unorthodox movement
production of natural odors fused with perseverance

an empress in a world of evaluation
of capability through droughts of pain

she wore a tiara of magnolias
before declaring to be queen of heartbreak
with a smile in lipstick
of bloodshed against a softened face
she understood negotiation of self for validation
was never to be offered on silver platters
in appeal for no man

ii.
kindness was a burned bridge
it was in chills of moonlight he rebuilt
essence as an emperor from flaws in waves of thoughts

he wore a crown of bones with pricks
before declaring to be king of distress
hardness in reflection of eyes revealed less tension
on a face from understanding
compromise of self for pleasure was expensed
on gold plates for no woman to indulge in

rock bottom.

living in depression with a lean on addictions
taught how to support yourself after a fall
on hard surfaces from shoulders you couldn't lean on
drunkenness was reaction to feeling insufficient
that soul begged for a secure hold
from something, anything away from resonance
in how hard you were on yourself

so focused on hating yourself to see in reality
you didn't disappoint
stop giving in to lies told to yourself

clouds expelled breaths of long hours
in composition to days, for once
it was understood words weren't just weapons
but armor too
icebergs of emotions formed within
mentality defrosted chills
in build up over the course of years

dust storms didn't dissolve, advancement traveled to new days
as haze of beliefs, only to be welcomed
with an open mind
advices were best given away without taken in
change was hard to keep cultivated within

for rebirth to bloom like a bouquet, it'll demand water
when clouds expel breaths of long hours
in composition to days, train yourself
to remain unmoved in crevices of growth

keep moving.

there will come a time when support
from solidity beneath your feet
is no longer needed to watch recollections
wane farther to a distance
you will hang from stationary stars
corded to power their glow, for feet
can't ever tread upon depths of relentlessness

meditation.

in waking to cleaner slates
shame couldn't build homes here
in being reminded to revisit drawing boards of time
sometimes, paces became too staggered in spaces
without quiet times fitted in

footprints of existence couldn't engrave large imprints
without walks of guidance, indentations
couldn't scar breaths in usage as fuel within me
moving forward seemed impossible when away
from this peace of mind

don't strengthen attachment to tangible things
only to realize life was best enjoyed
when steeped in experiences
investment on time comes with no refunds or exchanges

soulful.

live energetically
despite repeated knockdowns
a spirit in rise above chaos
can never outgrow newfound joy
in cemetery of what was
happiness kissed curves of wine glasses
much like softness in bends around corneas

this is freedom from bondage

vainglory.

"i wasn't brought up to romanticize disney movies
i found chivalry in literature
when hands pampered delusions, there used to be
muscle in arms to tear moons from her breasts
and squeeze sunrises to stifle darkness from sneaking in
i couldn't keep exposing this heart
when compassion ran away
i hop scotched this frame of mind to find it again
in retrace of steps to gift someone else
for them, i understand others may have failed to deliver

these women seem misguided
by self entitlement worn as crowns
they can keep handsomeness
with words like gravity to unravel desires
i'd rather be ugly in nakedness to show you
how realness is foundation to longevity, we
can watch beauty fumble to stay relevant
when aging in wrinkles of jadedness
eventually becoming sexless
these days, the majority aren't playing for keeps" the beast asserted

dream chasers.

remains of confused remnants were stripped
like dangled hangnails, before blowing
study how they lean forward in conviction
towards a path they're heading for without second thoughts

affirmations taken are directions out of shadows of doubt
each one teach one, i know these words will reach one
to someone in process of building one to benefit everyone
there's reliance in spoon feeding
like a child following parents footsteps
a symptom for unseen missteps in elders
to better whatever situation they deemed a settlement

observe, learn, live
let live

redefinition of a kiss.

lips crept ladders of steep collarbones
followed by a tongue in descent to sweep deep trails
across soft grasses in pastures of skin
this came from wanting you to stay
wanting you to stay
so your heart wouldn't fall like a meteor

crowned flames were a head piece
fingers struck hair like matches
to burn in your entrance of slow kisses
impulse pushed comfort deeper

"there's vulnerability in this body
succumbing to spasms by your hand
be genuine when forging me in fire" i warned

her sense of self.

i.
you were byproduct of stars in illumination of joy
a fresh scenery for cameras to reflect
brightest one shining among over developed skies
now on a run towards validation, you can't see how
you're more than a pump station
in rotation for men with fixations
older days are dependent on decisions
made from youthful years, an empty pot
is left when you allow many men
to plant seeds after plowing
without first tending to your soil
or soul, a woman majorly felt drained from body of emotions

ii.
you, the most beautiful ballerina
balance desires for lasting memories on lashes
strength holds up posture of a future mother
mindful in who is chosen for a father, embers
whisper between cheeks from mouths
in conversation from two worlds, where love is most warm

iii.
you won't be stationary to value architecture of family
if accustomed to moving with replacements
of prefabrication in quenches of sexual nature, that's foolery

prowess.

i.
keep passion in a churn
you're the forgery to hammer battle gear
strength knows no reduction
it's only projected
goals were slaughtered by fierceness
when you could have chosen life in numbness

ii.
each morning at cracks of dawn
you redressed in iron before walking in sunbeams
of boosted radiation in confidence
you will lose excess weight in hate
upon exercising appreciation for self
who was gorgeously woven by a creative mind
don't allow people to take turns
steering that precious vessel of yours
free of charge

commitment.

you're my first thought upon waking
reminders of you travel off road like jeeps in freedom
this, an afternoon rejuvenation, come evening
is appreciation awaiting your return home
roughest of days couldn't penetrate
love in extension far from lust of godly bodies

night draws nigh after our long workdays
in amazement by our growth, am i
who believe love to be mutually giving
and equally cherishing
these eyes close in anticipation for a day
not to be promised
it's in this darkness, i'm reminded of why
you shouldn't be taken for granted

ode to parenthood.

i.
curves of mouths stretching upward
amplify stories of you being the rock in this family
for better or worse
nurture was professor for unconditional love

ii.
i wish it were possible to hike slopes of ups and downs
to document your regained strength through tight kinks
where you felt withdrawn to a shadow
you live as though there's a difference between
being planted verses buried
and it's the world's duty to remind itself
you're a seed waiting its turn to bloom without permission

iii.
parenting required unending stamina
you never ran out of endurance
determination was heaven sent
i can't ever voice how much power was felt
when you said you believed in me

iv.
we have not always been close, you and me
we stripped love to simplicity
of putting the other above oneself
we've both come to know rejection through heartache
you won't carry those emotions to your final years
diversity doesn't have to divide us
when we speak the same language of love through action

what you've poured in this world
will come back to greet later in yours
you won't find dread here to take care of you
only a returned heat source
i've machined to duplicate yours
for everything i've acquired has been because of you
someday, i'll give it back
this, i promise

unchained.

thoughts glanced through windows
but never stepped foot beyond opened doors
they window shopped the skeleton
of a soul carved out

this centered cage was a clothes line to hang dryness
you sliced off bits of me to keep
yet discarded makeup of identity, energy
took up definitions among hallowed shells
essence became malleable, i fell gullible to sexual influence
to sever branches was homicide
we were all on the same tree, soul ties
was in every bit spiritual

feelings covered themselves modestly
for prying eyes unclothed me
we can never know strangers
if hearts maneuver invisibly

we pressured each other with timelines of forever
only to hurt immensely, this
a pain we cared not to deal with
when it became easier to ignore

my spirit graduated from its budding phase
an umbrella of emotions in flow of syllables
i ripped apart hate
so others could read peace from a relaxed pen
which remained in a process of purification
joy was uncovered within, for everything
on this plain has an end, tension

desired to persevere where destruction was its survival

no more, do i utilize eyes for beauty upon sight
instead, ignite me in hymns from a light inside
a natural influencer
to indicate goodness in storage within
this will eventually surface outwardly
death to self was to win at being right within

let it be.

no more laying awake at night
counting deaths of escaping stars, i held old days
on pedestals of new ones, but
how could they be new if still smelling like you?
no more letting you consume me so much
i lose track of writing the past, there's no
brainstorm of a future
destruction felt compulsive
was this obsession? or inability to let go?
but oh, how in low moments
we fail to see our own nudeness

once you read between some lines
you reject being a breeding ground for pettiness

some hid their spots, but skin
restructured trauma in rebellion as their establishment
battles within proved a smoothness came
from roughest cuts, true healing

so keep your chest empty of negativity
to watch treasures store up
harness no apologies for space taken up
in sequences of just being yourself

drainage of sensitivity.

bent among scattered lights of dark gazes
were weep songs from concaved ribcages
shadows were exposed in flexibility
between navigated false meanings
dreadful lines marked youthful faces
slits spoke like wet mouths to pin innocence
against cold walls
with strength from tongues in heated lust

we embarked upon severed spines
of trust like building blocks
yet on impulse, we veered off course
mistakes shared likeness of sound
with silences from deteriorated ruins

these ears are no longer sensitive
to sounds of broken glass
for this mind has built mirrors in loudness
of lonely reflections

righteous.

i pray to be surrounded by nothing but light
to wield as fire in this fight
to seek life, as i strive
to live a meek life

i wish to speak life
a humble, seemingly antique life
an always give thanks during the week life
to stay up
keep my head up and own up
even when it feels like i hold a drained cup

genuineness never stops, train yourself to cheer up
in focus away from things thought to have become broken
it's atrocious to have felt this hypnosis
what if a lost soul was misdiagnosis?

it's in praises of sturdiness
fire bellows in brilliance, this is why
i desire to be a recipient
a witness to such overlooked experience
of giving thanks to this universe
to accept it, not protest it, as a melanated being
of creation, you should know why

out of bounds.

hours draw breaths in minutes
slower, in breezes of dark nights
i scale blessings like batman in action
dividing pasts like a fraction
it's no longer part of my equation
exes, ex-friends were all the same
sensations no longer felt
this headspace was a coffin
for silenced thoughts, more so
with a freezer for a torso
with overgrown frost

forsaken in a hearse was this heart
it was a curse to chase when you were the one hurting
i take nothing for granted
spinal cords were not shifting blocks
to morph to staircases to other home bases

staying motivated by what i go through
with deeper analysis on life
i no longer vocalize pain soothed in self love
this i heard was the only way
when envy disguised as plain love

it's easy to hoard selfishness
until a dying wish becomes present in reality
for rewind on fulfillment from money and possessions
it was all a trap to keep you aching for more
it's why the rich will overdose despite having it all
everyone on the outside is now dead to me
no more tiptoeing on eggshells because we discarded mindfulness

no more living in lack of awareness to give into unstable emotions
no more being used as supply when living with this pineal eye

suffocation of life.

i.
often times we have desires to acquire something
not all can remain persistent in means to acquire it
why isn't the ground work
for longevity taught as cause and effect?
where you call to collect over time
because you exchanged distractions for clearer visions?

ii.
i never cared to allow regret
to room in chest spaces with installed payments
these days, i let no one cause me distress
everyone seems to be on a spiritual killing spree
with validation as a prize
there was no willingness to serve loyally
but everyone wanted to be served faithfully
what mattered more was fulfillment of desires
i can't help but question, if out of habit
we neglect as a side effect from parental abandonment

iii.
build a home away from bunkers of flesh
to retain a new house smell
in ways to preserve yourself
don't feel defeated if lungs can still inflate pain free
nothing was lost if in the end, you can still breathe

reign.

a wise man once told me
"craving freedom is symptom of a deprived mind
like a journalist, record visions as extremists
by killing laziness between blank spaces
if thoughts mimic explosions
you're an activist for what's revealed
from a soul in personification on paper
now a terrorist to distractions, passion
is enough to excel in this life through creativity, see
people have been doing this for centuries
they just had to escape penitentiaries of their own mind
be your own editor but don't erase your life's thesis
practice doesn't make perfect
it makes you more critical
of a craft you developed because you stayed habitual
stay true to you and never do as they do
i suspect this is how your mind gets lost these days
following others like religious rituals
as individuals, we need to look out of others
and into ourselves
to coast blessings from birthrights of our own lane"

self-infliction.

i found happiness when i stopped having expectations
expectations are what hurt
in this life so short with afflictions
self-infliction is felt when living by someone else's decisions

before the mouth opens, use ears to hear
before stroking canvas with pens, ponder a bit
before spending anything
you must first earn something
before praying, forgive
before hurting, feel
before hating, love
and before quitting, remember to try

each day is a push towards the greater you
problems can be self-made, but responsibility
barricades like a nightshade, once you come into yourself
you're homemade

new family.

i refuse to allow
matters of this outside world
to control levels in the bandwidth of emotions
within this temple

healing within my version of a dynasty
remains as the bigger picture
indefinitely

new history.

i'm breathless every time i see
forever in your smile
my reflection in your eyes
remind of how we've kept trying through some cries

love was never something to birth and die
like an angel, you taught me how compassion multiplies
and that this route of expression
is our only version of togetherness

simple living.

i've simplified this life of purpose
from experience we share through passion
to always learn lessons of joy

the selling of souls is to stay pacified towards information
that bleed us out internally while amusement remains glorified
but if electricity is needed to power distractions
why is it hard to believe light
powers you, the real entertainment?

open your veins and arteries like doors and windows
let in moonlight to walk in your own right
never be afraid of the night

change what's consumed
detox from programming which lowers spiritual immune systems
you're more than a symptom to this life, a fluke
we must build each other up to create impact like a nuke

now let there be light

If you enjoyed this book, please kindly leave a review.
Visit www.javierrhoden.com for more art.

Milton Keynes UK
Ingram Content Group UK Ltd.
UKHW020626070823
426447UK00017B/1192